Rescue on the Outer Banks

by Candice F. Ransom
illustrated by Karen Ritz

On My Own

HISTORY

M Millbrook Press/Minneapolis

To Taylor, again—C. F. R.

*For my brother John, who still wants to be
a fireman when he grows up—K. R.*

The photograph on page 46 appears courtesy of the North Carolina Division of
Archives and History.

Text copyright © 2002 by Candice F. Ransom
Illustrations copyright © 2002 by Karen Ritz

Millbrook Press
A division of Lerner Publishing Group, Inc.
241 First Avenue North
Minneapolis, MN 55401 USA

For reading levels and more information, look up this title at www.lernerbooks.com.

Library of Congress Cataloging-in-Publication Data

Ransom, Candice F., 1952–
    Rescue on the Outer Banks / by Candice F. Ransom ; illustrated by Karen Ritz.
        p. cm. — (On my own history)
    Summary: Sam Deal and his horse, Ginger, help an African-American lifesaving
crew rescue shipwreck victims off the coast of North Carolina in 1896.
    ISBN 978-0-87614-460-2 (lib. bdg. : alk. paper)
    ISBN 978-0-87614-815-0 (pbk. : alk. paper)
    ISBN 978-1-57505-184-0 (EB pdf)
    [1. Shipwrecks—Fiction. 2. Wild horses—Fiction. 3. Horses—Fiction. 4. African
Americans—Fiction. 5. Outer Banks (N.C.)—Fiction. 6. North Carolina—Fiction.]
I. Ritz, Karen, ill. II. Title. III. Series.
PZ7.R176 Re 2002
[E]—dc21   2001-000052

Manufactured in the United States of America
9-44761-4899-9/18/2017

Author's Note

The islands off the coast of North Carolina are called the Outer Banks. They are also called the "Graveyard of the Atlantic." In the days before ships used powerful gasoline engines, storms often drove ships ashore on the islands. Many sailors and passengers lost their lives in the angry seas.

In 1874, the United States Life-Saving Service built stations along the beaches of the Outer Banks. Each station was run by a keeper and a crew of six surfmen. These men rescued shipwreck victims. African Americans usually held the lowest rank. As "surfmen number six," they took care of the horses and cooked for the crew.

In 1879, the white keeper of Pea Island Station was fired. The supervisor decided to hire an African American, Richard Etheridge, to replace him. He had been surfman number six at another station. No white surfmen would work for the new keeper. So Etheridge put together an African American crew. Pea Island became the first all-black life-saving station.

This is the story of what happened at Pea Island one stormy October night. Ten-year-old Sam Deal was not a real person. But he could have been one of the boys who longed to be a surfman on the Outer Banks.

October 8, 1896

Pea Island, North Carolina

Sam Deal nudged Ginger
over the sandy dune.
The horse bucked a little.
"Easy, girl," Sam said.
He hung on to the rope around Ginger's nose.
Until last spring, Ginger had been wild.
Sam had caught her and tamed her
all by himself.

On the other side of the dune,
the ocean sparkled.
The water was calm.
But Sam had seen the ocean rage.
The Outer Banks were famous
for wild horses and wild storms.

Hundreds of years ago,
a ship had wrecked here.
The small horses on board swam ashore.
They ate sea oats and grew rough coats
and ran wild.
Ginger's ancestors had been part of that herd.

Sam spotted the surfmen.
They were practicing
with their life-saving equipment.
Keeper Richard Etheridge lifted
the line box from a cart.
Surfman Wescott waded out into
the water with a pole.
For the surfmen's practice,
the pole would stand for the mast
of a wrecked ship.

Two surfmen lugged a small cannon
off the cart.
Sam slid off Ginger's back.
"Can I help?" he asked.
He tried to lift
one end of the cannon.

"That's too heavy for you,"
said Surfman Bowser.
"Little boys like you should stand back."
Little! thought Sam.
He wished he was big like the surfmen.
He wished he was strong
like Keeper Etheridge.

11

The men buried the anchor in the sand.

They fired the cannon.

A line soared from the cannon over the water.

Surfman Wescott grabbed the rope.

Men on shore tied the other end to the anchor.

Then they attached a breeches buoy
to the rope.

The breeches buoy looked like a life preserver
hooked to a pair of canvas shorts.

Surfman Wescott pulled the breeches buoy
across the water.

"Time's up," called Keeper Etheridge.

Sam knew the drill had to be
finished in five minutes.

"Who wants to ride?" said Etheridge.

"Me, sir!" he said.

"All right, Sam Deal," said the keeper.

Sam swam out to the pole.

Surfman Wescott helped him into
the canvas shorts.

They held him safely above the water.

The surfmen on shore hauled him in.

If he were on a sinking ship,
the surfmen would rescue him this way.

"Good work," Etheridge told his men.

"You too," he said to Sam.

Sam grinned.

He tried to make himself taller.

"How's your surf pony?"
said a member of the crew.
"She big enough to haul the cart yet?"
The other surfmen laughed.
"Ginger's a horse, not a pony," said Sam.
He knew the men were only teasing.

Wild horses like Ginger were small.
The surfmen used strong, sturdy mules
to pull the equipment carts.
But Ginger was lots smarter than a mule.
Sam was sure that Ginger would be
a fine surfman's horse one day.
As he rode home, he thought,
Someday I'll prove what Ginger can do.

October 11, 1896

Sam turned Ginger's nose
toward the rain.
It was a bad night.
He should go home,
but he wanted to patrol.
Every night, the surfmen walked
up and down the beach.
They looked for ships in danger.
Sam liked to ride along and help.

Water dripped down Sam's rainhat.
Wind tore at his slicker.
When the weather was too foul,
Keeper Etheridge sometimes
called off the patrols.
Sam should hurry home.

Fwoosh!

Sam heard a sound over the lashing rain.

He saw a flash of red high in the sky.

A distress rocket!

A ship must be in trouble!

Sam urged Ginger toward
the life-saving station.
Through the heavy rain, he saw a light.
A surfman in the lookout tower
must have lit a lantern.
The surfman would use it
to send a signal out to sea.

Fwoosh!

A second rocket streaked

in the distance.

A ship was down for sure.

Nothing would make Sam Deal leave now.

He wanted to help rescue the survivors.

The station doors swung open.
Keeper Etheridge and his crew
rolled out the carts that held
the equipment and the lifeboat.
The men harnessed the mules.
Sam knew that the two carts
weighed over a thousand pounds.
The crew set off in the howling night.
The mules struggled in the deep, wet sand.
Big waves crashed over the beach.
The men had to stop often
to avoid the water.
Sam followed on Ginger.
"Go back, Sam!" one of the men yelled.
But Sam would not.
He had to help.

No one could see through the thick fog.

At last Sam spotted the wreck.

A three-masted schooner had run aground.

It was stuck on a sandbar, far from shore.

The surfmen unloaded the cannon.

Water flooded the beach.

They could not bury the sand anchor.

They could not use the
breeches buoy.
The surfmen pointed to the lifeboat.
Keeper Etheridge shook his head.
No man could row a boat
on those raging waves.
Then Sam heard cries over the howling wind.
It sounded like a child.

Sam jumped off Ginger's back.
The horse's rough coat smelled
like wet leather.
Freezing water swirled around Sam's knees.
The ship's sails had been ripped away.

The cabin was bashed in.
It looked like it had been hit
with a giant hammer.
Sam saw people on the deck.
The ship's crew held on to a woman
and a little boy.

"What'll you do?"

Sam asked Keeper Etheridge.

But he was too busy to answer.

Etheridge told two surfmen

to tie stout ropes around themselves.

Strong Theodore Meekins knotted a line

around his middle.

Then he tied the line to the second man.

"Swim out to the wreck,"

Keeper Etheridge told them.

Sam gulped.

Surfmen had to do tests,

like diving into deep water

to bring up a heavy weight.

But swimming in a storm like this

was dangerous.

"Take an extra line," Keeper Etheridge yelled

above the wind. "Hurry!"

Waves battered the schooner's hull.

Soon it would break apart.

The two surfmen leaped into the choppy sea.

On the beach, the others dug in their heels
and held the swimmers' line.

Sam held his breath
as the surfmen went under.
Then he saw their heads rise
above the hissing foam.

At last the men reached the ship
and climbed on board.
They tied the little boy to
Theodore Meekins's back.

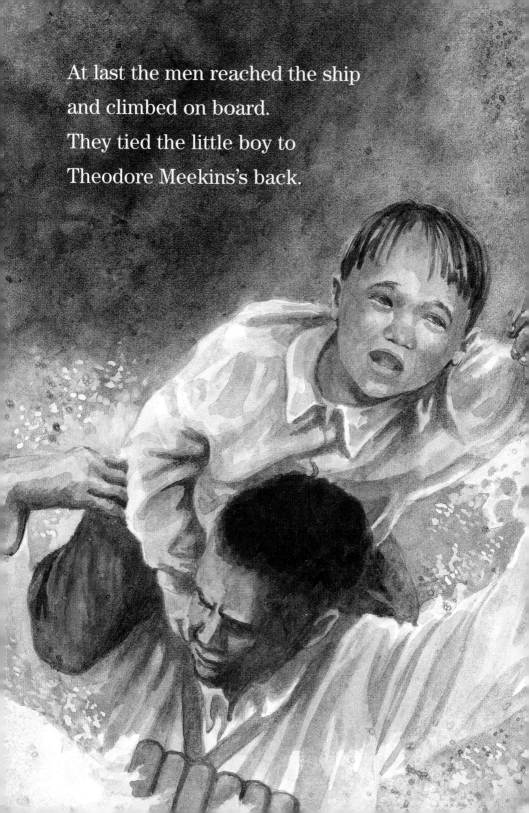

The men struggled back to shore.
The boy's face was white.
His teeth chattered from the cold.
Sam helped Keeper Etheridge
wrap him in a blanket.

Two more surfmen swam out to the wreck.
This time they carried back the child's mother.
She told Keeper Etheridge
that she was the captain's wife.

Her husband's ship was the
E. S. Newman.
There were seven others to rescue.
It was going to be a long night.

Suddenly Sam saw a way to help.
Climbing on Ginger, he rode closer
to the *E. S. Newman.*
The little horse was not afraid
of the churning water.
"Stop, Sam!" called Keeper Etheridge.
Close enough, thought Sam.

The surfmen were returning with
the next victim, a sailor.
The man gasped for air.
His legs buckled as he tried to stand.
"Get on behind me!" Sam said.
The sailor was grateful
for the ride to the cart.

For six hours, teams of surfmen
swam out to the wreck.
They brought back all nine survivors,
including the captain.
Sam helped carry them
to the cart on the beach.
Not a single life was lost.

At the station, Keeper Etheridge
gave the survivors food and dry clothing.
"You are all heroes," said Captain Gardiner.
He was thankful that his family was alive.
"It's our job," said Keeper Etheridge.

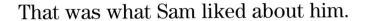

That was what Sam liked about him.

He did not brag.

Sam was proud of the surfmen.

He was proud of Ginger, too.

His little horse had braved the rough waves.

Ginger had done what the mules could not.

The next day, Captain Gardiner brought the
ship's name plank from the wreck.

"My way of thanking you," he said.

"You all deserve medals."

Sam thought so too.

"Sam Deal," said Keeper Etheridge.

"You and Ginger make a good team."

The surfmen cheered and patted Ginger.

Sam felt as tall as a lighthouse.

Maybe someday he would be

a surfman on the Outer Banks.

The Pea Island crew in about 1900. Keeper Richard Etheridge stands at the far left.

Afterword

In 1915, the U.S. Life-Saving Service became the U.S. Coast Guard. The stations on the Outer Banks were still used for search-and-rescue operations. Eventually the stations were shut down as modern rescue methods were developed. Pea Island Station closed in 1947.

The U.S. government awarded medals to many white life-saving crews. But the surfmen of Pea Island Station never received any recognition for their bravery. Richard Etheridge and his men were most likely over-looked because they were African American.

In 1995, eighth-grader Katie Burkart wrote a letter to President Bill Clinton. She believed the men deserved a Gold Lifesaving Medal. President Clinton and Admiral Robert Kramek of the U.S. Coast Guard agreed. In 1996, Admiral Kramek awarded gold medals to Richard Etheridge and the crew of Pea Island Station for their brave rescue of the *E. S. Newman* passengers and crew.

It was nearly a hundred years after that stormy night in October 1896.

Websites about the *E. S. Newman* Rescue

Pea Island Life-Saving Service
http://www.uscg.mil/hq/g-cp/history/STATIONS/PEA%20ISLAND.html
The U.S. Coast Guard historian's office offers facts about Pea Island
Station and its history.

Pea Island LSS Crew's Gold Lifesaving Medal Rescue
http://www.uscg.mil/hq/g-cp/history/11%20OCT%201896.html
Also by the U.S. Coast Guard, this site tells the story of the
E. S. Newman rescue.

U.S. Life-Saving Service Heritage Association
http://www.uslife-savingservice.org/
This organization works to preserve the history of the U.S.
Life-Saving Service. Here you can read a timeline of life-saving
throughout world history.